Author's Note

Since these psalms were first written,
my own spiritual and religious development
has led me to avoid reference to God
in exclusive, masculine terminology.
However, in deference to poetic style
and in respect for the original authenticity
of these writings, I have chosen, in some instances,
to leave the language in its original form.

Edwina Gateley 1992

PSALMS

OF A

LAYWOMAN

EDWINA GATELEY

ANTHONY CLARKE
WHEATHAMPSTEAD
HERTFORDSHIRE

SOURCE BOOKS
TRABUCO CANYON
CALIFORNIA

First published in the U.S.A by Claretian Publications in 1981
First published in Great Britain by Anthony Clarke in 1986, and reprinted in 1988
and 1989.
This edition published by Source Books and Anthony Clarke, 1992 and reprinted 1993

Source Books
Box 794
Trabuco Canyon CA 92678
USA

Anthony Clarke
16 Garden Court
Wheathampstead Herts. AL4 8RF
England

ISBN 0-940147-00-9 (USA)
ISBN 0-85650-072-0 (UK)

Printed and bound in the USA by KNI Inc., Anaheim

For Maureen

CONTENTS

FOREWORD

People always told me there was little market for religious poetry; it was with some trepidation therefore that the first edition of Psalms of a Laywoman was published in 1981. The response and the complete sale of the first edition convinced me that people are hungry for personal and authentic "God-experiences". I believe all of us are blessed with these experiences and that our lives are popping with miracles and revelations. The problem is we do not discern or recognise them.

In this book I have tried to share my experience of God and miracles and revelations. Many are painful and shot with struggles and loneliness (God's absence is as powerful as God's grace). I have not doctored or edited my poetry; most of it has been written over the years as an authentic expression of personal experience and my search for God. I have recorded both joys and sorrows in this search, I have shared my darkness and my light. That in itself is a risk. But I believe it is worth taking if it leads other Christians to become more aware and confident of their own experiences of God and their own potential to seek and embrace the living Spirit within them.

I hope my book gives testimony to God's action in the world today and God's call to all of us to become fully and actively involved in calling forth the Kingdom throughout the earth.

THE
PSALMS

STIRRINGS

There is a strange,
Untouchable, unseeable
Thing in me.
It hungers,
Grasps, strains
For something
I do not know,
Far beyond—

It stirs,
Turns, disturbs.
It brings with it
Unknown things,
Unidentified longings.
It reveals a vision hazy,
Far, far,
Very far away.

INVITATION

In the face of your love I'm a coward to give,
Your demands, your totality make me afraid,
Weak to respond to such strength and such fire
Trembling to pursue a love so true.

Desiring, yet dreading, drawn reluctant
To a flame devouring, all consuming,
Taut with resistance against the love
That demands such total giving.

Tempting—the joyless comfort of darkness.
Tempting—the undemanding shadows.
Oh! Let me run and let me hide
From this love which will embrace my all!

Night of indecision, night of pain
Dancing and taunting and laughing before me.
Oh! In the comfort of your shadows—
Let me curl and let me sleep.

WAITING GOD

This is a way
Strange and beautiful,
Full of wild hope
And quiet fear
At the inevitability
Of it all.

For God is there
And God will watch,
Tirelessly wait
All my life
For me, for me
To come ~~to Him~~.
And the way is there—
Though only dimly comprehended.

But God—this patient God,
Will never
Give up.

HOLD ME FIRM

It is hot and clammy,
The night is thick
With the heat,
And in the silence
God is present—
Captures and envelops me,
Like the heat.

Hold me firm,
My God.
Infuse me
With your Spirit.
I have not the strength
Nor the courage,
To love as You would have me.
But as You cannot leave me,
So build me up
And use me.
Make of me what,
From time to time,
I dream of
With a sadness great
That I can only dream—
Make me into a lover,
My God.

continued

Show me Your ways
With patience,
Show me Your Light,
Half veiled,
Show me Your Life
That I might live.
Abba —
Never release
Your hold on me,
Strong, firm, tender,
Though I laugh before You
And am unaware
Of Your Beauty and
Your Pain.

5

UNSURE

O Lord, that I may see a little,
That though I seem confident and sure,
I be aware that I also can be wrong,
That I might never be so sure of myself
That all doubt is swept aside.
For I am human and should be prepared
To be brought low,
To be found mistaken.
O Lord,
Don't let me see confidence in You
Where it is only confidence in myself.
Don't let me seek a new way
Only because it challenges me
And may not be right for others.
Give me, Lord,
The wisdom to see what
You will
And not what
I want.
What You have planned and not
What I have dreamed.
What You wish to build and not
What I wish to achieve.
The wisdom, O Lord,
To see the difference.
The courage and humility to accept—
If I am wrong.

DON'T LET ME SAY ENOUGH

Tax me not, my God,
Beyond my strength,
Or the strength,
Cold and impenetrable,
That visionless men
Would armor me with.
O God, this is
A lonely banner
You would have me hold.
How many times has its weight
Gripped me in loneliness and fear?
Will they not see, O God,
Beyond the banner?
Will they not see, O God,
Beyond the power and the glory?
Will they not see, O God,
Beyond the laughter and the charm?
O God! Will they see
Nothing more!
I am weary, God,
Of tears and anguish in solitude.
I am weary, God,
Of the visionless men.

I am weary, God,
Of the empty glory and acclaim
Churned out unthinkingly
Without understanding.
I am weary, God,
Of your banner.
Where now is your Spirit in me?
(O God—hold out Your hand!
Take this from me
Or hold it firm with me)
Where now,
Your joy and peace?

Enough, again?
Must I say Enough?
Don't let me say Enough!

FEELING ALONE

Sometimes God leaves us alone
Or leaves us to feel that
We are alone.
We wonder what it's all about—
Are we wasting our time—
Are our eager efforts,
Laughable, doomed
To fall and crumble on
Stony ground?
With enthusiasm and childlike
Hope
We step forward—hands
Outstretched
To grasp the Infinite.
Ungraspable
Intangible
Elusive.
We stand
Disappointed, crushed
With outstretched hands
Falling . . .
Empty.
Abba!
Father!

8

THE FOUNDATION

Now the struggle is over,
We have it,
We have succeeded.
What was abstract,
What was theory,
What was a dream,
Now is reality.
We have it in our grasp,
It is here—
Before us.

Why then, why O Lord,
This fear?
This hesitance and doubt
Which plays before me
And tempers the strong conviction
Which once was mine?

Those who questioned and doubted
Now have trusted me.
They have agreed.
They have put their faith in me.
Here lies my fear,
In fulfilling
Their trust and hope
In me.
O Lord, it weighs so heavy
Upon me.

continued

Lord, don't leave me,
Let me find Your strength
In my doubts,
Let me find again
The faith which inspired me.

Now, O Lord, it is a reality.
Make my faith real enough
To do the work
Which now lies before me.

HOLDING ON

Has the time come, then,
That alone now and quiet,
The very silence of my room
Shrieks out and threatens me?
The ground that once
Was firm and strong
Beneath my powerful stride
Shudders and shifts
And shakes my being.
I retreat into my room
Like a fugitive,
There to fall back,
Numbed and tired
To search for strength
To face that which
I do not understand.

My God—equally present
In darkness as in light,
Stand by me!
Allow me, yes, to suffer and
Be hurt,
But not to be broken or destroyed.
Allow me to be bruised,
But not my spirit to
Be overcome.

continued

HOLDING ON *continued*

I know of suffering and
I do not fear it.
I only fear my strength
To carry it.
I ask not to escape from
The doubts and the pain,
I ask that I might carry them
With grace,
With hope,
With love.

CALLED TO SAY YES

We are called to say yes
That the Kingdom might break through
To renew and to transform
Our dark and groping world.

We stutter and we stammer
To the lone God who calls
And pleads a New Jerusalem
In the bloodied Sinai Straits.

We are called to say yes
That honeysuckle may twine
And twist its smelling leaves
Over the graves of nuclear arms.

We are called to say yes
That children might play
On the soil of Vietnam where the tanks
Belched blood and death.

We are called to say yes
That black may sing with white
And pledge peace and healing
For the hatred of the past.

We are called to say yes
So that nations might gather
And dance one great movement
For the joy of humankind.

continued

We are called to say yes
So that rich and poor embrace
And become equal in their poverty
Through the silent tears that fall.

We are called to say yes
That the whisper of our God
Might be heard through our sirens
And the screams of our bombs.

We are called to say yes
To a God who still holds fast
To the vision of the Kingdom
For a trembling world of pain.

We are called to say yes
To this God who reaches out
And asks us to share
His crazy dream of love.

11

RESTING

The spirit
Which once rebelled,
Fought furiously
And swept all aside
In its determination—
Now sleeps.

The hunger,
Though not satisfied,
Remains gaping hollowly,
Silently, within.
The restless life,
Undisciplined spirit,
Which clamored for freedom
Now is tamed,
Now gently
Lies and hides,
In patient waiting.

STAND BY ME

Living God—stand by me.
Hold me up.
Be my strength when
I am tired
My inspiration when
I am bored
My life when
I am listless.

Living God—I cannot always
meet the standard
Expected of me,
Cannot always be
The personality
I am known for.
Abba, when I fail,
Abba, when I stumble—

Stand by me.

13

I AM TIRED

I am tired, Lord,
Nearly all day
I have felt tired,
And yet not been able
To stop—
Except, I remember,
For ten minutes
To think of You.
And even then,
I thought of all
But hardly of You,
And watched the clock
To see when
I could get up and go again.
I am dizzy with the people,
The notes to remember
And all the confusion
Of many things
To do and think about.
Lord—there's so much
To remember!
All afternoon and evening, Lord,
I had a headache—
But even that did not lead me
To think
Of You.
I snatch each night
The midnight hour,
The only one that is mine,
To turn to You
Only to tell You, Lord,
That I am tired.

PRAYER IN THE OFFICE

Where is my solitude now, my God?
Where the peace, the stillness
That I might find You?
Where the silence in which to hear
Your voice, my God?
Is it that I must seek You out
Anonymous,
In the constant stream of callers?
That I must hear Your voice
In the telephone calls and
Conversations?
Is it that I must look for You
In the endless stream of traffic which
Passes my door?
Where are You, my God,
When I have no solitude
In which to stop,
To turn and look at You
In silent greeting?

15

THIS MOMENT

Snatch now a stolen moment
From the hurtling days that,
Undistinguished by their sameness,
Pass without a murmur or a mark.

Make something of this moment,
Let it live through awareness
That its pulse will beat still
When the day itself is dead.

Rejoice in this moment!
Steal away in glee to a secret corner
Like a thief rewarded.
This moment is mine—mine all alone.

16

SILENT GOD

This is my prayer—
That, though I may not see,
I be aware
Of the Silent God
Who stands by me.
That, though I may not feel,
I be aware
Of the Mighty Love
Which doggedly follows me.
That, though I may not respond,
I be aware
That God—my Silent, Mighty God,
Waits each day.
Quietly, hopefully, persistently,
Waits each day and through each night
For me,
For me—alone.

EUCHARIST

Kneel like a stone,
Empty, unfeeling,
And murmur:
I love you.
Watch the movements,
Unmoved,
And murmur:
Take my life.
Eyes with no shine
Follow the hands
On the altar,
Watch the Host raised—
Plead for significance,
Heads are all bowed,
Responding to the prayers.
Do they feel, these people?
I love you.
Do you know I'm here?
Unfeeling, unmoved, cold.
Do you know I've come?
Waiting, watching, hoping.
Do you remember me?

I thought I loved you once.
I've come again.
The priest offers our prayers.
Yes—here we are.
I love you.
We are going to share
In the Feast.
We are going to drink of
The Life-Blood.
Follow mechanically, step by step.

continued

I'm here.
The Sacred Host is eaten.
Empty, unfilled.
I love you.
Do you know, God, that
I'm here?

It's nearly over.
But I haven't finished—
You haven't answered!
Didn't I get through?
But you are within me.
I love you.
Wait . . .

No—it's over.
The Mass is ended . . .
They're all leaving . . .
I love you.
Didn't you hear me say. . . ?
Empty, bewildered, hurt.
Kneeling.
Shattered.

DARKNESS

There is no light in my darkness
No spark to break through the void
Into which with crushing swiftness
I am cast without chance to protest.
Oh! Once I walked in joy and daylight
And laughed at the dawn and the night,
I delighted in God's presence and
Skipped in the light of the sun!

But now I fall before the sunlight
And sob at the memory of joy,
The laughter that danced before me
Echoes and mocks me far away.
Where once I walked with powerful stride
I creep and hide in shadows
And where once I boldly gazed,
I shade my eyes in shame.

No strength to cry—to sob: Enough!
Unable, even, to whisper.
No more to reach and find firm hold,
Only empty chasms around me.
No more to stand on ground secure,
All! All is swept away!
And I, a naked child in the night,
Lost, bewildered, alone.

No Father now, to hold me up,
No Lord to strengthen me,
No Spirit to breathe a touch of life
In this night of desolation.
And the deepest, darkest pain of all
Shrieks wildly through my anguish:
The love is gone! The joy is done!
Curl up—and die alone.

19

SLEEPLESSNESS

Awake again—at the wrong time, Lord.
And I thought I was so tired tonight,
I thought I would drop off so easily.
Instead of that, completely unexpected
And uncalled for—
My mind is suddenly filled
With thoughts, ideas, plans.
They crop up, keep me alert,
Weary me with their persistence.
And in the morning, dear God,
I'll be dog-tired and irritable.
Will You be with me then, my God?
Will I remember then that I lay here
And thought of You
And turned to You
In my sleeplessness?
Will I think of You again
In my weariness
Tomorrow?

GLIMPSING GOD

I catch a glimpse,
Now and then,
Of God.
A swift passing
Sweetness
Which makes light
The hour, the day, the week.
Elusive, inconstant,
Yet never totally absent
From the hurtling days with
Their shadows.
I grieve
That such a beautiful
Awareness,
Like an unexpected visitor,
Comes infrequently,
Entertains briefly,
And passes
With a whisper.
Is lost then
In the laughter
And the music
Of the night.

SURRENDER

Into Your Hands, Lord,
This solitude,
Into Your Hands, Lord,
This emptiness.
Into Your Hands, Lord,
This loneliness,
Into Your Hands—
This all.
Into Your Hands, O Lord,
This grief,
Into Your Hands
This sleeping fear.

Into Your Hands, O Lord—
What is left,
What is left
Of me.

NEW LIFE

I suffered, and now there is joy,
I was lonely, and now there is comfort,
I was desolate, and now there is warmth,
I was empty, and now there is fullness.

The years and months of struggle dragged on
And plunged me into dark solitude,
And now, why now,
Do I see the light and feel the warmth?
Is it that my despair reached its depth
And God, in pity, said: Enough?
Where was my soul then
When my spirit was so dead?
And now there is a relief,
An almost tangible gratitude
That it is over
And a spark of life and love
Is born from nothingness.

This will not last forever.
But thank you, God,
For living again,
For letting me know and feel
Your life and presence in me.
And if this hope should die again,
Let me remember
The years of emptiness
That passed.

Stay now, God,
A little longer.

LEAVING AND FOLLOWING

Gently,
My soul quietly,
Undramatically
Is disturbed.
Who, what,
Whispers to my soul?
Will this God of mine
Not forget,
Nor be satisfied?
What more, now,
Does He ask
To intrude upon
My comfort and serenity?
I have given
This, that, and the other.
Will this God of mine
Not rest
Till He has
My soul and life-breath?
But how I treasure,
In silent satisfaction,
My life-style
And all its accoutrements!
How happily I possess
My flat in London,
Decorated so tastefully
And so well.

How I delight in
The comfort and pleasures
And company
I have gathered around me!
What would You
Trade these for,
My God?
Will You continue
To run Your Finger,
Gently,
Over these smooth waters
Moving around me?
Will You disturb
My tranquility
Longer, my God?
Or will this be
A passing shadow
Moving mysteriously
Over my soul
And receding,
Into nothingness?

THE BELONGING

Presence ever yet around me
Strength unasked for by my side,
Love unwarranted, before, behind me,
God within me, God without.

Held still tightly like a child
With the freedom of a woman,
Certain, sure and more aware,
God is mine and I am His.

Seen a Love—total, powerful,
Though the vision is yet half-veiled.
God closer, nearer, breathing,
Claiming me, as I would Him.

SILENT PRESENCE

I thought that God
Had come to me.
That after the wild delights
And the suffering and the joys
And the pain and the hopelessness
Of the years—
That God
Had come to me.
That after adventure and achievement,
Pain, despair and death,
God
Had come to me.
Yes—with relief and mild surprise
I met my God again.
And then I saw,
Oh, fool, I saw!
That God had suffered
The pain and hopelessness,
Had shared the achievements and the joys,
That God,
All enveloping,
All compassion,
Had been there in silence
All the time.

26

THE DYING

You didn't tell me how bad it was.
You didn't tell me that I nearly died.
Amidst all the work, the fury, the haste,
With all the excitement, the plans, the hopes—
I nearly died
A death not known, not believed in—
That would have been the horror of it.
Nothing told me.
No one spoke.
And in my dying that no one saw,
I was applauded.
All was mine—the laughter, the smiles,
The adulation,
Stored and gathered
They were mine.
Only rarely, my spirit disturbed,
I would be sad and wonder.
And then with dash and scorn
I would dismiss
This weakness.
See my work! See my achievement!
Don't these speak for me?
When so many smiled upon me,
So many admired,
How could I die?
But in the years You disturbed me, God;
All were sure, except You.
And no one told me
I was dying.
If You had left me
I would have died.
But not known it.

You would not be challenged
Nor cornered,
And nobody told me
I was losing.
I lost, God.
What pity, what despairing love
Drove You to come to me?
What, to disturb me at dawn
And in the darkness,
To awaken me with tears and despair?
To touch me then and haunt me with
Your presence?
And, taken by surprise,
I was afraid.
I—the one who laughed and won,
Was afraid.
I did not come to You.
You came to me.
What had I done, my God,
That You could not
Let me go?

It was You, God.
It was You
Who told me
I was dying.

IN SOLITUDE

There is a peace here which surely must be rare
For it is very deep—it soaks into the bones.
It steals in with the moon-filled night
And envelops this tiny stone hut—
Gently, silently.
Peace. All sleeps. Enshrouded.
Listen—listen! Silence sleeps.
Even the cockroach crouches unmoving
And the flame in the oil lamp is
Still—still.

My spirit stirs with wonder
God creeps in—almighty presence—
Into this domain of solitude
And deeply, deeply enters every
Crevice and corner.
Gently, imperceptibly
Holds my soul suspended
In His mighty silence.

THE HERMITAGE

It is dark in this rough stone hut.
The desert night is silent and utterly still,
There is only a slight hiss from the oil lamp
Which lights this little corner.
Shadows fall on the oil drum—full of water—
By the wooden door,
And a cockroach crouches beneath
The huge tin trunk crammed with blankets,
Sugar and rice.
My clothes—limp and creased—
Hang from a steel rod wedged between
The crevices of the stone wall.
A blue plastic mug, a torch and a
Crumpled Kleenex tissue
Are set beside the sleeping bag
For the night.

It is beautiful, and lonely here,
Nakedly simple with only the bare necessities
To live.
There is a kinship between my soul and these
Sharp but protective stones that make this
Basic shelter—this refuge—comforting and safe.
I share a peace and a oneness with
The oil drum, the tin trunk and the
Bits and pieces scattered around—insistent symbols of
Human habitation.

continued

THE HERMITAGE *continued*

We've been set apart from the everyday action
And interplay of life.
The city—the town—and all their feverish movement
Exist now as memories
And we, the oil drum, the tin trunk and the
Bits and pieces
Are thrown here together
In this corner—this tiny living corner—
In the vast and silent Sahara.

TEA IN THE DESERT

Wandering, alone, through the desert.
Sun shrieking heat,
Sweat pouring and dripping,
Rocks, barren and hostile
Sheltering
The brave desert flower.
And I—solitary beating heart
In a vast and empty land
Wandering, wandering, seeking
A lost and lonely God.

Beyond the rocks
A smell of goats
Hanging thick and sweet
In the still air.
And there, standing defiant against
A thousand miles of sand,
A woman
Burnt brown, clad
In sweeping black and
Colored beads.

We walk to meet,
To cross
The centuries and the nations.
Eyes, black, shining a lost
And ancient wisdom
Speaking the naked horrors
And splendor of
Uncompromising solitude.

Smile. No words.
Shattering the barriers of language.
Hands touch,
Brown and cracked,

continued

White and smooth,
Clasping and joining
A thousand cultures.

Walk together to her home
A rough and sturdy shelter
Of rocks and goatskins.
Squat on Tuareg rug laid out
Proudly on the sand.
Smile. No words.

Eyes, searching, speaking
A million unknown words.
Tea. Thick, hot, sweet
Prepared with love and care
In an old tin kettle
On an open fire.
Sip. Smile gratitude.
Smile. No words.

Woman of the desert.
Woman of the West.
The world brought together.
Peace and harmony established.
Rivalry and hate abolished.
Black and white.
The lion and the lamb.
Smile. No words.
Tuareg woman.
English woman.
Sharing the Kingdom
Sipping tea
In the vast and lonely desert
With a found and
Living God.

JOY

Let the hills and the plains tremble,
Let the silent sky be shattered
With my cry!
Let the hot stones stir
Beneath my feet
And the startled lizard
Lie transfixed—attentive and amazed—
At the sound of my call.
Let the black desert beetle
Scuttle and hide in new-discovered fear!
Let the mountain birds swoop
Into the darkened crevice of the rocks
As my lonely voice
Breaks and shatters the desert's solitude
Cry—cry—aloud my voice!
Before it let the mountains crumble,
Let the heavy desert heat be swallowed up
In the breath of the child that cries
Aloud to the God of heaven!
Cry, cry my voice!
Conquer and master the dry, lonely desert
Drink the solitude, absorb the silence
And look upon your God.

Hush—be still—
Let the voice fall and be swallowed
In the hot white sands
For the Lord speaks—
The voice of the Lord unfolds
Like a gentle mantle
On the desert plains—
The voice of the Lord
Strokes the mighty mountains,
Embraces—envelops

continued

The child—alone and wandering
On the great plain.
The voice of the Lord
Penetrates the sun-red rocks
And reaches to the roots of the
Brave desert flower.

Then the child—
Mighty crier,
Bows and falls before the Lord.
And the voice—now a whisper—
Gasps, suspense-like—before the
Wondrous Presence;
Lord—your servant!
And the heavens—the great heavens
Are silenced,
The vast desert listens—suspended,
The desert creatures hide and crouch
Beneath their rocks
And the voice—the tiny voice
Of the child
Fades
Before the all-absorbing glory,
And the gentle stroke
Of a mighty, mighty God.

RENDEZVOUS

It was real and it was a dream
It was a dream and it was real.
The day had been light, gold
With a glorious sun sweeping its warmth
Over the plateaux and the hills
Soaking its timeless heat into the
Very stones
And I laughed, and my heart laughed,
In joy, like a child, I scrambled
Up the mountain
To the top. The very top.
". . . Lest you dash your foot
Against a stone . . ."
An adventure—an adventure—
An adventure with my God!
"Look God—see God—
How beautiful!"
At the top I rested on a rock
And laughed at the
Glory all around.
The Pinnacles!
The forms—the colors—
The vast vast spaces!

Hush—be still. . . !
Was it real?
Or was it a dream?
I could no longer laugh,
A great stillness held me
A mighty arm enfolded me
Thoughts and dreams were suspended, and lost
In the mountain air
And I?

continued

I too, lost . . .
A great love had caught me,
Held me
And I was awestruck and amazed
Emptied of all else but
The vibrance of a love
Which consumed even that which it filled.
Aware, hardly, that my heart beat—
For it waited on Him—
Startled, then hushed
By this total and swift capture
Afraid to beat
Lest this great lover flee!

Glorious, beautiful!
And in the pregnant silence
The mighty mountains stirred,
Turned,
And looked upon
The Sacred Rendezvous.

UNION

Moon creeping steadily, throwing light
On my darkness.
Heavy night, burdening my soul with the weight
Of its emptiness.
And I—
Alone before the silent moon,
Startled by the living pain
Its light revealed.

Soul, naked, bereft, sobbing in
Exposed solitude,
Creep, confused and dismayed to
The silent house—refuge of
A silent Lover,
There to crouch and cry—
Wounded.

Moon, pitying, filters through
Its rays,
Falling and playing,
Eliciting no response, no playful finger
To chase its light.
O, curl, curl, child!
Who would die from too much love
And tenderness
Now withdrawn.

No sound, no cry,
Only a soul's anguish
Heaving silently.

continued

Even the moon rays
Now transfixed,
Reluctant to play and dance
Before such grief.

Startled—Startled now!
In thunderous rush
A Mighty Force
Sweeps, suspends, saturates all
In suddenness stunning!

Fall! Fall!
Loved before the Lover!
Fall! Fall!
Wounded before the Wounder!
Fall! Fall!
Oh, lonely seeker before the Sought!
For now, Oh, now God comes!
Now in a mighty rush
God sweeps upon me,
And His gentle breath
Lifts my swelling soul
To where
I cannot know
And where
I cannot live.

Swift and silent the capture.
Paralyzed.
No movement.
No whisper.
Only a Mighty Sense of Being
Carried into being.

The great Wave
The great Power
Now suspended
Holds and soaks my soul
In vibrant, vibrant Life.
Pain beautiful
Holds me
Poised
Lost
Found
In Sacred Union.

Hush, moon!
Hush, silent night!
Lest in your very
Stillness
You disturb
The rapture
Of this pregnant hour.

HUSH

Hush, hush, My loved one,
That you might hear
My music
In your soul.

Still, still, My loved one,
That you might feel
My life breath
In your veins.

Sleep, sleep, My loved one,
That you might wake
To my touch
Upon your cheek.

Die, die, My loved one,
That you might live
In my Spirit
Deep within you.

Come, come, My loved one,
For you must know—
I have waited long
For you. . .

34

LET YOUR GOD
LOVE YOU

Be silent.
Be still.
Alone. Empty
Before your God
Say nothing.
Ask nothing.
Be silent.
Be still.
Let your God
Look upon you.
That is all.
He knows.
He understands.
He loves you with
An enormous love.
He only wants to
Look upon you
With His Love.
Quiet
Still.
Be.

Let your God—
Love you.

35

ABBA

Abba, Father
I love You!
Abba, Mother,
I thank You.
Abba, Father,
I am not afraid.
So let me walk
Your way
Wherever it may lead.
Only Lord—
Go before me.

THE FIG TREE

I saw the fig tree blossom afar
Ripe and rich against the sun.
And, hungering for its delicate taste,
Towards it I did run.

This fruit is mine! This fruit is mine!
See it hanging on the tree!
And heavy burdened though I was,
I hurried to taste and see.

And as I clambered up the hill,
Hands reaching out in hope,
My feet dragged heavy beneath me
And I stumbled on the slope.

I could not leave my pack behind,
My clothes, my food, my drink,
And I held on tightly to them—
Beneath their weight to sink.

I fell in tears of anguish
And sobbed into the ground,
As I realized in my misery
It was mud, not fruit, I found.

And in the silence of my pain
I lifted my head to see,
Humbled and empty-handed,
The rich fruit of the tree.

RELUCTANT WRITER

Do I presume to touch
The divine?
And squeeze from this
Limping soul
A spark and light
To flame and kindle
Others?
And dare I reach into
An abyss
To drag forth
A diamond?
And would I—
Small soul—
Reflect the Infinite
Out of my own
Dark nothingness?
Is my pained cry
An echo—
Drenched in emptiness?
Or is it a tiny,
Tiny whisper
Born of an anguish
Not my own
And straining for a birth
That can only come
From darkness and
Defeat?

SPIRIT-POWER

Power-moving, creative,
A force without origin or source
Only a mighty whispering Presence
Heaving the mountains and
Splitting the earth.
Blind—we cannot see,
Nor smell, nor touch
But there is an awakening—
An expectancy,
Threading the soul to the beat
Of heart and pulse
And charged with breath
Divine.
Restless, stirred,
We strain to glimpse
The Infinite
Beating and breathing about us.
But the Power-moving—is creative only
In our fragmentedness
Moves the mountain
Because we fall beaten
Before it
Splits the earth
Because we sob in despair at
Our frailty.
Power, moving creative—
Seize!
And let us shudder—
In Your sacredness.

THE WHISPER

Wakeful hours
Full of silences and murmurings
Province of the gods.
Spirit hovering
Calling
To communion.
Silence, sweet,
Sweeps my soul into
Consciousness.
Awake, my soul!
For the Lord calls
And His whisper
Shatters my being.
There is no time,
Only existence
Which is because
God is
And struggles to return
To the Creator Force
Which gave it being.
Life calls life,
Love gently touches,
And love,
Reawakened from
Its darkness
Responds and reaches out
To the Source which
Feeds it.
Awake, my soul!
For the Lord calls
And would meet and
Love you
In the darkness of
These sleeping hours.

CALLED TO MINISTER

There is an anguish
In action
After having loved
Solitude.

Called to minister,
Called to lead,
And knowing that the Lord
Has enriched me with
These gifts.

And yet—
Deep and dark and hidden
So far, far within me—
Something cries out
For fulfillment,
An insistent, inexplicable
Yearning
For aloneness,
For a vast desert
Where my soul can chart
Its search for God.

Called to minister,
Called to lead,
And yet painfully reminded
In the last late hours,
That I was most and
Deeply happy
Alone and lost
In the desert sands
In search of a
Lonely, loving God.

RESTLESSNESS

My spirit is restless
I feel myself straining and grasping for
Something
Which has
No form
Nor can be articulated.
I only know
That a power moves within me
And disturbs me in the day and
In the night,
I only know there is a call
I cannot hear,
A vision
I cannot see,
And the pain I feel is
Inadequacy—
Deafness—
Blindness.
Deaf and blind
I sob,
Alone,
In a pain
That cannot be shared,
A cry
That cannot be heard.

Blank, colourless, formless
Seeping—saturating.
Strange force which defies
My grasp and
My control.
And I will cry
Against
This half-death!
This night
Without star!
For I do not want
To die. . . .

THE NOT YET BORN

Volcano—Volcano.
Bubbling rich red.
Steaming.
Spirit—creation
Bursting. Bursting
For release and life.

And I must
Carry you
Hot and aching
Within me
Until your time
Is come.

Mysterious,
Lonely gestation,
Formed in darkness.
Fed and nurtured
By a life and spirit
Breathing gently, powerfully
In my soul.
Hush. Silence.
The time is
Not yet.
Now is only
Slow murmurings and
Gentle stirrings.
Oh! Not yet born!
But how you live!

I love you, Volcano.
I love your
Sweeping pain and
Thrusting, tentative movement.

I love you, Volcano,
As you sleep and wait
Within me
For your life.
And for your death.

LETTING GO

It is time to go.
I can smell it,
Breathe it
Touch it.
And something in me
Trembles.
I will not cry,
Only sit bewildered,
Brave and helpless
That it is time.
Time to go.
Time to step out
Of the world
I shaped and watched
Become.
Time to let go
Of the status and
The admiration.
Time to go.
To turn my back
On a life that throbs
With my vigor
And a spirit
That soared
Through my tears.
Time to go
From all I am
To all I have
Not yet become.

I will not cry
But tremble
At the death
Within me
And sob
Tearless
At the grief
That heaves
My soul.
Time to go.
Lonely, brave
Departure
That stands
Erect and smiling
Whilst my very being
Shudders
In utter nakedness.

MEMORIES

It was here, in this great and grey cathedral
That you surprised and captured me—
A child in school tie and blazer
Held awestruck by the vast silence
And cool dampness of these pillars and
Frescoed walls,
Gold angels' wings, set in rows against a
Thousand stars,
Virgins, saints, and martyrs clasping lilies and
Jeweled staffs . . .

And there, hanging before me by the
Fourth pew,
The great silent crucifix bearing
Down and breathing upon me
Its lonely mystery.
Statues solid and secure, speaking
Calm and peace
To my staring eyes seeking to
Catch them out in movement.

Massive sacred altar for the blessed!
How I loved the ritual and the liturgy
Its incomprehensible movements and language—
Secret cult of which I was a silent part.
And this great grey cathedral
Was mine!
Mine to wander in and be amazed
Mine to cry and whisper in
Awed by a mighty sense of being.

It was here, in this great grey cathedral
That you surprised and captured me.
It was here
So young, so naive, and so ready to love
That you stole from your shadows
Upon me
Clasped me
And whispered from the great stones and pillars
Echoing past the rows of angels' wings
And reaching out from the sacred altar.

Yes, it was here, here
That you broke through your splendid fortress
And bent to kiss
An amazed and wondering child.

THE BURIAL

They buried a monk today.
Uneventfully, simply,
They laid his body in the ground
Wrapped in a cowl and shroud.
But the earth trembled.

I did not know the man,
He was only a name,
But the bells rang deep
And full of grandeur.
And the earth trembled.

The abbey was cool
And the mighty stones
Spoke the voice of timelessness,
And in their great stillness
The earth trembled.

The monk had been a soldier,
The dry desert had gulped
His sweat,
And beneath his clumsy army boots,
The earth had trembled.

He had cried alone in the desert,
Seeking his silent God
Amongst the tanks and the guns
And the emptiness.
And the earth trembled.

They buried a man of God today
Who had found life in desolation
And joy in death.
They buried a monk today.
And the earth trembled.

THE SHARING

We told our stories—
That's all.
We sat and listened to
Each other
And heard the journeys
Of each soul.
We sat in silence
Entering each one's pain and
Sharing each one's joy.
We heard love's longing
And the lonely reachings-out
For love and affirmation.
We heard of dreams
Shattered
And visions fled.
Of hopes and laughter
Turned stale and dark.
We felt the pain of
Isolation and
The bitterness
Of death.

But in each brave and
Lonely story
God's gentle life
Broke through
And we heard music in
The darkness
And smelt flowers in
The void.

continued

THE SHARING *continued*

We felt the budding
Of creation
In the searchings of
Each soul
And discerned the beauty
Of God's hand in
Each muddy, twisted path.

And God's voice sang
In each story
His life sprang from
Each death.
Our sharing became
One story
Of a simple lonely search
For life and hope and
Oneness
In a world which sobs
For love.
And we knew that in
Our sharing
God's voice with
Mighty breath
Was saying
Love each other and
Take each other's hand.

For you are one
Though many
And in each of you
I live.
So listen to my story
And share my pain
And death.
Oh, listen to my story
And rise and live
With me.

CALLED TO BECOME

You are called to become
A perfect creation.
No one is called to become
Who you are called to be.
It does not matter
How short or tall
Or thick-set or slow
You may be.
It does not matter
Whether you sparkle with life
Or are silent as a still pool,
Whether you sing your song aloud
Or weep alone in darkness.
It does not matter
Whether you feel loved and admired
Or unloved and alone
For you are called to become
A perfect creation.
No one's shadow
Should cloud your becoming,
No one's light
Should dispel your spark.
For the Lord delights in you,
Jealously looks upon you
And encourages with gentle joy
Every movement of the Spirit
Within you.

Unique and loved you stand,
Beautiful or stunted in your growth
But never without hope and life.
For you are called to become
A perfect creation.
This becoming may be
Gentle or harsh,
Subtle or violent,
But it never ceases,
Never pauses or hesitates,
Only *is*—
Creative force—
Calling you
Calling you to become
A perfect creation.

A DREAM I HAVE NOT DREAMT

There is a dream
I have not dreamt
A vision
I have not seen.

There is in me
A fearsome longing
Deep as primordial waters
And rooted in
The very womb
Of earth's fire.

There is in me
A life not become,
Stirring and reaching out
From the dreams and terrors
Of dark history.

There is in me
A fire not kindled,
Glowing like a lone
And passionate sentinel
Awaiting the dawn.

There is a dream
I have not dreamt
A vision
I have not seen.

RESURRECTION

The Fishermen

Part I
We were fishermen, simple people
Who only asked for a decent living
And a fair deal.
But life was rough;
We never caught enough fish
And our meagre income was
Heavily taxed by the Romans.
We hated them—oppressors that they were.
But then one day this guy
Came along—a strange fellow
By name of Jesus.
There was something about him,
Magnetic, I suppose.
Anyway, he knew how to speak and
How to work wonders.
The crowd loved him
Followed him everywhere they did.
We were flattered that he chose us
To be his friends and followers.
We could hardly wait for the Kingdom!
We were sure it was about to come
And we little people would be free,
No longer oppressed and beaten down,
Oh, no, *we* would have the power then!
Jesus filled us with hope
For liberation.
So we believed in him,
Trusted him.
Followed him.
Proud and flattered and excited.

But then, you see,
Our hopes were shattered.

continued

Crucified

For our hero—
Our hero—
Well . . . they did him in.
He died upon a cross.
It was so awful. So embarrassing.
We were ashamed to see our hero
Beaten and destroyed.
Oh, what a letdown!
We ran, like rabbits here and there,
Bewailing our misery,
Humiliated by our pain and our betrayal.
He betrayed us, you see,
That was obvious.
Got us all excited.
Gave us great hopes.
Then smashed them all in
And us at the same time.
He was never very clear, of course,
We never really could figure him out.
A funny guy.
He never minced his words when he knew
Things were wrong
And shouldn't be.
He was always putting his foot in it,
Lashing out at injustice and oppression.
He wasn't scared to say what he thought.
But we liked him.
And he loved us.
We believed that
In spite of his odd ways
And embarrassing behavior,
He'd win in the end.
Yes, there was something about him.
Till they did him in.

72

And then it all fell apart. *Good Friday*
What was he on about?
He fooled us.
Such embarrassment.
We were the laughing stock.
All that blood and spit and pain
Didn't fit our notion of
God and Kingdom and power.
Jesus fooled himself and fooled us too.
Betrayer and betrayed. Simple fools!
So we hid, scared and humiliated.
Ran like hell we did.
We'd nothing left.
We abandoned him
Like he'd abandoned us.
We could hardly look each other
In the eye.

But then after it was all over, *Resurrection*
And we were just mooching about
And miserable,
Something happened.
It was amazing.
Suddenly he was there!
We saw his Spirit
In the life around,
We heard his voice
In the voice of another,
We felt his touch
In the touch of another.
Our world turned over.
We couldn't understand just then,
We only experienced and believed.

continued

From our pain and misery
Came life! Suddenly surging up
Bubbling and so, so free!
And we said:
Jesus-man-hero was killed
And Jesus-man-hero
Is alive!
And then we knew, we knew
That he was man
Because they killed him,
And we knew, we knew
That he was the Christ
Because God raised him up,
And then we knew, we knew
That he was us and we were
To be him.
His life began to speak anew
As we heard again
What he had preached and taught—
Freedom, justice, love.
All the things people couldn't take,
For they are not what we have built.
We have our own gods.
And so, you see, they killed him.
They had to.
He was a threat. Troublemaker.
Sign of contradiction.
When we saw him again,
It began to make sense
Because we realized
It was just the beginning.
We had to take over then—
Carry on the work he'd started.
What a job! What a path!

Oh, what a crazy God
To go so far
To prove his point.
No glory and no triumph.
Only faith that came
Through pain and death,
Faith in our God—Man-God
Who taught us such a lesson—
Such a lesson.
Turned us upside down.
We see now.
The path of Jesus is ours,
That same love and action, once his,
Now ours,
But they'll not like us
Any more than they liked him.
We too will be a sign of contradiction
To selfishness and greed.
We too, a threat to
Establishment and peace.
We are all this because we believe.
We believe there is life.
And we believe because
God raised him up.
We know, you see.

Part II

And what of us?
I cannot speak of us,
I can only speak of me
And say that I too have seen
This Jesus whom they killed.

continued

And I too have heard all
He preached and lived by.
It was once taught to me
In a classroom as a child,
And I squirmed and played and waited
In boredom for the clock
To strike my freedom.
And when the freedom came,
I ran out to the world
Excited and full of joy.
God was simply a reasonable idea,
Somebody had to create it all—
That was logical enough.
Jesus was a bit of a legend.
But I thought of him, now and then.
Sure—he was a good guy.
But he was dead.
Well, he never really lived
For me, you see.
But they told me I should believe.
So I said I did and even
Thought I did.
I prayed to God and Jesus—
That was the right thing to do,
They told me.
But people and life were
More interesting than
A benevolent, boring God, and a dead Jesus.
So I leaped into life
And into the world.
Jesus was dead.
And I was alive!

But something happened to me.
I looked and saw pain and despair
In the world into which
I had leaped
So sure and proud and triumphant.
Reaching out to the pain I cried:
This must not be!
This cannot be!
(But you see, Jesus was dead.)
Then something happened to me.
It was amazing.
Suddenly he was there!
I saw his Spirit
In the life around,
I heard his voice
In the voice of another,
I felt his touch
In the touch of another.
My world turned over.
And I knew, knew without a doubt
That Jesus was alive,
And I knew that he was the Christ
Because God raised him up
For I had seen him.
From my own pain and my own despair
I had seen him,
And in my Yes, though anguished,
Was Yes to all that he had stood for,
Lived for, died for.
The cross, the death—
I saw the reason why,
Foolish, foolish reason.
Amazing.

continued

But I believed, you see, because
They killed me too.
I had my death and
He raised me up.
I live now as he does.
I live to proclaim what
He proclaimed—
Life in death, liberation from
The prisons that we have built.
And I am free,
Because I died and now
I live.
First, first we must die to
Really understand,
For if we follow his way
We must die.
There really isn't any other way—
If you're serious
About the Jesus
Who lives.
Because he died, you see.

THE ANOINTING

There were no crowds at my ordination
The church was cold and bare,
There was no bishop to bless and consecrate,
No organ music filled the air.
No solemn procession went before me,
No cross nor incense smell,
There were no songs nor incantation
And no pealing triumphant bell.

But I heard the children laughing
In the stench of the city slums.
And I heard the people sobbing
At the roaring of the guns.
And the stones cried out before me
As the sirens wailed and roared
And the blood of women and children
In the arid earth was poured.

There were no crowds at my ordination,
The church was cold and bare.
But the cries of the people gathered
And the songs of birds filled the air,
The wind blew cold before me,
The mountains rose and split,
The earth it shuddered and trembled
And a flame eternal was lit.

continued

THE ANOINTING *continued*

There were no crowds at my ordination,
The church was cold and bare,
But the Spirit breathed oh, so gently
In the free and open air,
She slipped through the walls and the barriers,
And from the stones and the earth She proclaimed:
Oh, see! My blind, blind people,
See Woman—whom I
Have ordained.

In the past few years a good number of people have urged me to write something on the beginnings of the Volunteer Missionary Movement. This is no easy task, perhaps because the events and the early struggles are too close to me, and more time and distance from the experience are needed. However, the following text gives a fairly clear, albeit brief, account of how the Movement began.

MY FAMILY

I was born in a small village near Lancaster, England, in 1943. I grew up during the war years, and I still recall the great care my mother took in counting out the ration coupons for sugar, tea, and various basic foodstuffs. We were a fairly poor, working-class family and I was a middle child—flanked by an elder brother, Colin, and a younger sister, Maureen. Both were better looking than I and, I felt, more intelligent. So I began to cultivate a competitive spirit from a rather early age. However, I did not have very much confidence in myself and failed to gain entry into the "better" schools to which my brother and sister went. In spite of this, and with the encouragement of Mrs. Bowes, my teacher, who did not want to see me spend my working life in the local shoe factory, I did well at school.

During these early years God broke through into my life in a powerful way, and I was very much aware of being "called" to some kind of service in the Church. As a schoolgirl I experienced the joy and surprise of being called by God. This left me with a determined, single-minded goal—to love and to serve this God and his people all my life. At the

age of fifteen I decided I wanted to be a missionary. Three years later, knowing that qualifications
were important in order to go to Africa, I went to
college to become a teacher.

"HELPING THE MISSIONS"

When I completed college in 1964, the Congregation
of the Sisters of Our Lady of Africa (White Sisters)
accepted me as a volunteer in one of their schools
in Uganda, East Africa. I spent my first year in
Uganda teaching postulants and sisters belonging
to an African congregation founded by the White
Sisters. But I soon discovered it was not easy to
be a lay missionary in a church that tended to see
mission only in terms of priests and sisters. I was
simply a "volunteer" *helping* the missions rather
than being an intrinsic and full member of the missionary activity of the church. Although it was a
rich and exciting experience, I soon realized that it
was not my calling to work within a religious struc-
ture into which I did not quite fit. On the other
hand, this first year's experience was an invaluable
and necessary preparation for the challenging and
difficult years which followed.

ON MY OWN: SCHOOL IN THE VILLAGE

In 1965 I asked the local Ugandan bishop, Adrian
Ddungu, if I could work for him in his diocese
wherever there was a need that I could help meet.
He welcomed my offer, and I ended up in the small
African village of Kyamaganda, eighteen miles from
the nearest town. I had over sixty children from
the ages of eleven to eighteen, and my task was to

build up a school from scratch. But facilities were poor and equipment minimal. There was no electricity or running water. The main diet was steamed banana with peanut sauce. Life was definitely very simple! But I loved the people and began to learn their language and their ways.

My experience in Kyamaganda taught me that mission was not all I thought it to be; it was not a matter of my going off (I, Edwina, a Western Christian) to the Third World to convert and teach "the poor." It was rather a mutual exchange and sharing of faith, gifts, and culture. The Ugandan people taught me many things. I learned from them when they reached out to strangers in hospitality and welcome; when I received their generosity, observed their patience, and witnessed their extraordinary ability to live fully the present moment. All this gave me a new and revitalized experience of God, who is found in all peoples and in all religions. During this time I was becoming increasingly aware of the very real conflicts and problems involved in being a lay missionary without the same credibility as the religious and ordained missionaries. As a layperson I did not quite fit into the missionary Church as it was then. I felt alone and alienated without the support of a community and with a deep awareness that I was considered somewhat "odd."

But life in Kyamaganda, with all its joys, was hard. Loneliness, poor diet, lack of facilities, and repeated attacks of malaria gradually weakened me and left me, after two years, feeling ill and insecure. I was increasingly doubtful as to how I could possibly spend my life as a lay missionary against so many odds. Sick and confused, I was forced to return to England in 1967. It was an awful time! I had come to love the people I now had to leave. I saw no future for myself at home. I had to work it all out and make sense of God's calling about which I was deeply convinced, but which, it seemed to me, had no place in the Church.

BACK TO ENGLAND: RECRUITING VOLUNTEERS

I went home to England to try to lead a "normal" life—to get a job and an apartment and "settle down" as all my friends had done while I was in Africa. I got a job—teaching eleven-year-olds in Liverpool—and I shared a bed-sitter with Brenda Morris, an old friend from my college years. But I never settled! I was continually bugged by my missionary experience in Africa. I was restless and disturbed. I could not shake off my deep desire to be a full and active minister in the missionary church. But how?

I hit upon one way of continuing my involvement—I began to put advertisements in the local paper to try to recruit men and women to go to Africa as volunteers. I was amazed at the response. Within a few months, the adverts plus a few talks that I gave to local groups, resulted in over a dozen people eager to be sent to work in Africa. I was elated! It was all done in a rather clumsy and unprofessional manner as I "interviewed" the candidates at train stations and restaurants and promptly sent them off to Africa in their first wave of enthusiasm. I had made contacts (bishops and missionaries) in a number of countries, and all I did was to recruit someone with the required qualifications, get an airline ticket from the prospective employer, and put the volunteer on an airplane!

The whole experiment did not last long. After a few months, problems began to arise, and the volunteers complained of loneliness, malaria and difficulties in relating to the people. I felt devastated by the fact that these, my first recruits, were meeting problems that they could not cope with and were therefore returning to England. I also felt frustrated and angry because I knew that their needs should be met, and were not being met, by myself and the Church. I began to realize that I was making a mistake—it was simply not right just to send people off to Africa without any preparation, proper selection, or ongoing support. I stopped advertising and wondered what to do next. I was very much aware that there was a real need for lay missionaries in the Third World, and that there were many people at home eager to respond to the needs. How could this be done effectively?

A CALLING BECOMES CLEAR

One day in January 1968, I came across the Vatican Council documents on "The Apostolate of the Laity" and "The Missionary Activity of the Church," and I read them. These two documents brought all my thoughts together in a way that made sense. They expressed in clear language the kind of ideas that had been vaguely going through my mind. They called for laypeople to gather together and organize their own forms of missionary activity under their own leadership, with proper preparation and formation for their members. The

Vatican Council documents stressed the ministry of the laity and called on the church leaders to recognize and to support such new lay ventures. My enthusiasm and hopes were renewed! The documents confirmed my call to be a catalyst for the emergence of a true and validated lay missionary movement in the Church. But I had no idea how I, a young teacher living in a bed-sit in Liverpool, England, could go about such a tremendous task.

A retreat was in order! So I booked myself for a retreat for five days where I could pray and reflect and decide what to do. The priest-director of the retreat offered to help me. He would give me a place to start and all the support I needed to launch a lay missionary movement. It seemed providential, and the offer was too tempting to refuse. I gave up my job and my room and moved to the far north of England to work with the priest and develop the new organization.

Soon, however, it became very clear that we had distinctly different ideas as to what a lay missionary movement and the spirituality it called for were all about. I believed it was important to challenge the laity to develop their own form of leadership, their own spirituality, and their own unique response to mission as lay Christians. I felt this so strongly that I had to leave this newly founded organization when it did not fulfill this need. The organization continued for a few years under the leadership of the priest and of one of the first recruits, who became the head of the new organization in my stead. The struggle and the disappointment of my first attempt to establish a lay missionary movement helped to clarify my ideas and thoughts. It also helped me to understand that any coming to birth involves struggle.

STRUGGLES

More than ever convinced that God was asking me to continue trying, I travelled around the country explaining my vision to anyone who would listen—sisters, laypeople, priests, and bishops. I gave talks, addressed various small groups, and wrote articles for publication. It was a hard time because as I was not earning a salary, I had to live on charity, accepting whatever money, food, or hospitality was offered. The hardest thing was the disbelief I encountered. The vision I saw so clearly was too unreal to some and too frightening to others.

It was also obvious that my first experience of trying to start a lay missionary organization and then leaving it (although this was not without advice from some leading missionary priests whom I had met) was seen by some as a failure. I was somewhat suspect as being unreliable and unstable. My reputation was not too good!

My efforts, my enthusiasm, and my passionate conviction seemed all to no avail. Why should they believe in me? Why invest money or property in me? By the end of 1968 I was dispirited and weary and ready to give up the whole dream. But I had a brainwave—I still had a hope left—John Cardinal Heenan of Westminster. An interview with the cardinal was my last attempt to win support for the foundation of a lay missionary movement. But certainly I was not prepared for the kind of questions the cardinal asked me: "Are you trying to start a religious order?" ". . . a secular institute?" "Will you take vows or promises?" I did not want any of these things! I only wanted to share with him my vision of a lay missionary movement, autonomous and free and led by laypeople. At the end of the interview, the cardinal declared that the Church was not ready for the kind of lay missionary movement that I envisaged. He considered that the time was premature.

THE FOUNDATION OF THE VMM

Totally disillusioned and wondering why God had treated me so badly, I returned to Uganda in October 1968. But in December 1968 I received a letter from Father Sean Murphy of the Missionary Institute, London—formed by seven missionary societies—saying that they had discussed my "case" and were willing to offer me a grant of £3000 and a house in London to begin the movement.

At that stage I was reluctant to return and to work in a Church where I had experienced so much struggling and suffering. However, the missionary societies were sincerely reaching out in support. So in January 1969, I returned to England and moved into the three-bedroom home provided for me by St. Joseph's Missionary Society in Mill Hill, London.

At last I could start to develop the movement of which I had dreamed for so long. The Volunteer Missionary Movement was named and founded in April 1969. I began advertising and recruiting; drew up a formation course; contacted bishops and missionaries throughout Africa—and the VMM was launched. The VMM began to grow and by 1975 had sent over 300 lay missionaries to work in more than a dozen countries in Africa, South America, and the Far East.

IN SEARCH OF COMMUNITY

As the years passed by, I began to feel the pressure of carrying the responsibility of the whole movement. By 1973 I knew that the VMM needed some kind of continuity in leadership involving more than just one person. I should no longer be alone. The idea of community emerged; I felt that if I could call together a group of returned VMMs and invite them to live and work together at the heart of the VMM, then the movement would be on firmer grounds, and at the same time we would be initiating a new expression of Christian community in the Church. These would be people who felt the need to live out their lay missionary commitment through VMM, on a permanent basis. I was excited and exhilarated by this new inspiration and began to share it with some of the VMMs. In October 1974, six of us gathered together and discussed the new dream. We began to save money, to make appeals for funds, and to search for a house where we could begin community. The money we raised was insufficient, so we borrowed a large sum from a sympathetic religious society and bought a four-bedroom home. There was a good deal of scepticism and opposition from a number of people who felt that the VMM should not be expending time, energy, and money on forming community. They could see the VMM only in terms of recruiting and sending out lay missionaries on a temporary basis. The idea of anything more permanent and ongoing was unacceptable.

Opposition mounted, my own leadership of the VMM was in jeopardy, and we were pressed to drop the whole venture of community. But the small group who had gathered was convinced it was right, and we decided to go ahead. So the embryonic community, unsure of its role and future, but very much inspired by the Spirit, at last began in January 1975. We had problems from the very beginning. Within a matter of months, the original six were only two—myself and Maria Gabriel. We felt an abysmal failure and somewhat of a laughing-stock. We were almost ready to abandon the whole idea, until Father Noel Hanrahan, a priest friend of ours, said: "As long as there are two of you, I will believe in you." We were encouraged. We prayed very hard for perseverance. Several people came and went. Then, at the end of 1976, a third member, Phyl Shannon, joined us and stayed. We rejoiced!

We invited returned lay missionaries to come and spend weekends with us and discuss the whole concept of community within the VMM. An encouraging number came, and much time was spent in good discussions and in prayer. But in May 1977 we had yet another setback. The premises that we had rented to hold all the VMM preparation courses became unavailable. We looked everywhere for alternative accommodation and failed. The only thing left to do was to hold the forthcoming course in the four-bedroom house where the community lived. Accordingly all the lectures, seminars, Masses, and socials were held in our home, and every day there were twenty-four of us for meals—sitting on floors and staircases wherever a space could be found! It was becoming clearer that community was essential if the VMM was to have cohesion, or ongoing support and stability. The role and the future of the VMM community were emerging.

LOOKING FOR A HOME

Accommodations for the VMM courses, for a base for the whole VMM, and for the new community became a critical problem. Twenty-four people in a four-bedroom semi-detached was just not practical! We prayed—and prayed! We pleaded with God to answer our needs. Time was limited, as we had another twenty-five lay missionaries coming for the next preparation course in November 1977. But no house appeared. I began to think that something must be wrong with the whole way we were approaching the problem. Surely, if we really believed that the VMM was God's work, then our faith should be strong enough to know that our needs were already answered before we knew them. I thought of the Gospel teachings concerning the lilies of the field and the birds of the air and of how the Father had counted every hair of our heads. Then I knew we should not worry or be anxious, but that we should begin to pray in thanksgiving for the house that was already waiting for us. So we thanked God for the large house and for the grounds that we could cultivate to grow our own food. Our prayer aroused some humour and scepticism among visitors and friends, who began to think we must be going slightly mad! "Where is it?" they asked. "I don't know," I answered, "but it is there—it is just a matter of discovering the location!"

By September of that year (1977) we were given a thirty-five-bedroom home in Hertfordshire, England, with four acres of land as a long-term gift from the diocese of Westminster. We rejoiced! The new community moved in, and returned VMMs and other people who were interested in the VMM came down from various parts of the country to paint, clean, scrub, fix broken windows, clean the overgrown land, and generally make the house habitable. In November 1977 the first VMM course was held at the new centre with the VMM community in residence. The community was to be the first of several VMM communities which later began to develop in various forms throughout the world. They are supportive, catalyst groups encouraging and coordinating mission and development education and activity in our home countries. The community at the centre in England is a strong core group involved in many activities such as retreats, conferences, Christian awareness workshops, and preparation courses for mission. Community members also travel the country giving homilies and talks and calling the laity to respond to their missionary vocation at home and overseas. Communities have also emerged in Ireland and Scotland, where the VMM is active and welcomed by the local church.

NEW STEPS

By 1979 the VMM was ten years old and had sent over 500 lay missionaries to work in twenty-six countries throughout the world. It was well and truly a strong and growing movement with a real sense of purpose and mission, a vigorous Christian community at its head, good formation programmes, and an active ministry. Truly the Lord had worked wonders! I felt I had given the movement as much as I could, and that it was time for me to leave and explore new possibilities.

Maria Gabriel and Su Hood agreed to take over responsibility for running the movement and to share the work, the struggles, and the ideals that had been mine. In doing this they allowed me the freedom to move on, and they took the VMM forward with fresh leadership and new ideas. For me this was an important step in the story of the VMM. I have a deep conviction that we should not hold on to a leadership position *ad infinitum,* but that we should always call forth new forms of leadership from the people of God. The Church, like any institution, is always in need of new life, vision, and renewal, which can only come from openness to the work of the Spirit in other people. We must allow new life, ideas, and leaders to emerge, whatever the cost to our structures, our little dreams, and our securities.

FROM THE SAHARA TO CHICAGO

After leaving the VMM community in May 1979, I spent three months in the Sahara desert. It was a time of solitude and prayer in thanksgiving and joy for all that the Lord had blessed us with and for the wonder of his work, which I had experienced so personally. It was also a time of listening and of preparation for my ongoing ministry in the Church. I now wanted to spend some time in study and reflection. The diocese of Westminster again responded, and I was given a grant to study theology in Chicago. In September 1979 I went to the Catholic Theological Union in Chicago, Illinois, USA, and completed my degree there in June 1981.

NEXT STEPS

The end of my studies led to the question: what next? The obvious thing seemed to be to get back into action and ministry. But I experienced a powerful drawing towards silence and solitude. I felt God saying: *Come apart, rest and listen for a while.* The call, though unexpected, was certain. It also corresponded with an invitation for the Volunteer Missionary Movement to establish itself in the USA and the free loan of a house and land for that purpose. It seemed to me that God was giving unusually clear messages.

Late in 1981 a small VMM community established itself in Yorkville, Illinois and I established myself in a hermitage in the nearby forest. I lived there for nine months. It was not, as I had fondly imagined it would be, a time of great peace and joy. On the contrary I was often exceedingly bored and frustrated. The *Listening* led to my becoming aware of a new call – that of beginning a ministry of love and outreach to the prostitutes and street-people of Chicago. Just over a year later, in January 1983, I moved to one of the poorest areas of the city and began to walk the streets and work towards establishing relationship of trust and friendship with the rejects of the streets.

I have come to know and love many prostitutes and to gain insights into their life-styles, their suffering and their experience of God. This continues to enrich my own spirituality and to stretch my awareness of God's amazing grace.

I am grateful that God has filled my life with many guides and teachers; the prostitutes and the street-people being amongst the most significant. As they are a source of inspiration to me, I hope my story will also be a story of inspiration for others and enable them to know and believe that God is indeed alive and well and scattering the kingdom all over the world.

**VOLUNTEER
MISSIONARY
MOVEMENT**

**THE SPIRIT
AND
LIFE~STYLE**

At a time in the
History of the Church
When passive obedience and
Reception of the sacraments
Was generally accepted
By the laity
As what being church
Was all about.
The VMM emerged as a
New and challenging movement
Calling Christian men and women
To respond to Vatican II's call
For full and active involvement
In the Church's life and mission.

This involvement has a
Double thrust:
To witness to God's action
Through Jesus Christ
In our world today
And to respond to the
Material and human needs of
The poor and oppressed.

We are first called and
Moved by the very Love that
Lives within us:
"The love of Christ overwhelms us. . . ."
(2 Cor. 5:14)

We who have received
The gift of faith
Calling us to
Personal conversion and transformation

Are also impelled
To share that love.
We who have received
The love of Christ through
The Spirit
Cannot contain it.
It must Reach out to others
Spilling out and
Touching the world in which
We live.
We believe that,
As in the Parable of the Talents,
(Matt. 25:14-30)

We have an
Urgent obligation to
Take Christ seriously enough
To share his mission and message
With others.

We are therefore
Sharers of the Good News
Through witness and love.
It is only through
The way we live, love, and serve
That we can truly witness to
The Christ who served
And invited us to do likewise.
Only in following His way
Faithfully
Dare we claim the name
Christian.

"If I, the Lord and Master,
have washed your feet,
you should wash each other's feet.
I have given you an example
so that you may copy
what I have done to you."
(John 13:14-15)

The spirit and calling
Of the VMM missionary is,
First and foremost, one of
Love and service in and to the world.
As laypeople we give a
Special witness
To the reality that all
The People of God
Are called to involvement.
In Christ's mission
All are called to serve.
Bishops, builders, and nurses alike
Must work together
Equally
Towards the coming of the Kingdom.
Mission is given
To us all.

We believe that
God calls His People
To harmony
Unity
And material interdependence.
We wish to dissolve
The barriers that divide
People and Church and nations.
We stand for oneness in
The body of Christ.

We commit ourselves
To the service of
Our God
To work among all people
Seeking to break down
All forms of injustice and oppression
And all inequalities
Of sex, status,
Color, creed, or nationality.

"And there are no more distinctions
between Jew and Greek,
slave and free,
male and female,
but all of you are one in Christ Jesus."
(Gal. 3:28)

Of its very nature
This mission cannot be
A temporary thing.
It is a total commitment
To the Gospel
And can be nothing less than
A way of life.

We take the Gospel
Seriously.
We must live it.
In giving ourselves
To each other
We will come
To fullness of love and revelation
Promised through Christ.

We follow Him with
That same trust and confidence
That He had in the Father.
For we know that
He is with us
And will not leave us alone.
"I shall ask the Father
and he will give you
another Advocate
to be with you for ever,
that Spirit of truth
whom the world can never receive
since it neither sees
nor knows him;
but you know him,
because he is with you,
he is in you.
I will not leave you orphans."
(John 14:16-18)

Our mission begins with
Our faith in the Resurrection
Which sends us out
In hope and love
To all the world.

We also wish to remain
As laypersons
Without any vows or promises.
To demonstrate
The ability of all
Men and women to be
Fully committed Christians

Whilst pursuing
Their own life-style
And calling in the world.
We do not separate
Our mission as Christians
From our day-to-day life.
We wish, rather,
To ground our own
Personal and spiritual growth
In striving
To become fully human
Within the context of
Our work and service in the world.
We represent a wide variety
Of charisms and life-styles
And may be distinctive only
By our commitment and openness
To the Spirit of the Lord.

Each VMM missionary
Takes personal responsibility
To seek and pursue
Fullness of Christian faith
In his or her own situation
And life-style
And aware of the
Support and prayer
Of the whole VMM.
Our task
Is to be true Christian witnesses
In the world
With that freedom and flexibility
That invites and embraces all.

We recognize that
We need each other.
We are a community-based movement
That stresses and encourages
The value of living together
Praying together and
Working together.
We believe that it is through
Our shared experience
In family and community
That we will truly
Grow together
In Christ.

"Above all the Gospel must be
proclaimed by witness.
Take a Christian
or a handful of Christians
who, in the midst of their own community,
show their capacity for understanding
and acceptance,
their sharing of life and destiny
with other people,
their solidarity
with the efforts of all
for whatever is noble and good.
Let us suppose that,
in addition,
they radiate in an altogether simple
and unaffected way
their faith in values
that go beyond current values,

and their hope in something
that is not seen
and that one would not dare
to imagine.
Through this wordless witness
these Christians stir up
irresistible questions in the hearts
of those who see
how they live
Why are they like this?
Why do they live in this way?
What or who is it
that inspires them?
Why are they
in our midst?
Such a witness is already
a silent proclamation
of the Good News
and a very powerful and effective one.
Here we have
an initial act of evangelization."
(Evangelization in the Modern World—
Paragraph 21)

Whenever possible, therefore,
VMM missionaries
Live together in small groups
Or renew and strengthen each other
Through visits, correspondence, or
Regular shared activities.

And so the VMM missionaries
Say *Yes* to Christ
And *Yes* to His mission.
We say *Yes* to the Church
Of which we are part
And we offer to the Church
Our service, our commitment
And the vision and the vigor
That we bring.

We must be
Men and women whose action
Is motivated and strengthened
Through prayer.
We gather together
To share our worship and prayer
Recognizing that Christ is
At the center of our lives
And that
As People of God
Celebration and worship
mean sharing and gathering.

Our prayers, as well as being
Shared and public,
Also involve
Personal and silent encounters
With the Lord
For which there can be
No substitute.

We learn to listen,
In all types of prayer,
Not only to the needs
Of our brothers and sisters
In the noise and action
Of today's world,
But also to that silent movement
Of God's action within us.
We bring together in harmony
The voice of the people and
The voice of the Spirit
And we strive
To respond to both.
VMM missionaries
Are listeners.
Our witness will be seen
When God's Spirit
Is so strong within us
That it is visible
In our lives and actions.

Christ was available to all
And reached out
To the poor, the sick, and the rejected.
He was one of them.
His mission is now ours.
Our mission is to be wherever
There is injustice
Of any kind.

"Wherever there are people
in need of food and drink,
clothing, housing, medicine,
employment, education;
wherever people lack the facilities necessary
for living a truly human life
or are afflicted
with serious distress or illness
or suffer exile or imprisonment
there Christian love
should seek them out
and find them."

(Apostolate of the Laity—Paragraph 8:4)

The majority of our world
Lives in hunger and want
Deprived of the most basic necessities
To live a decent human life.
Impelled and driven by
The Spirit of Christ
We cannot stand by unresponsive
To the needs
Of our brothers and sisters.
We must share
Ourselves.
They must have the tools
To enable them to develop
And be free.
They need the skills and the expertise
To bring out
Their own resources and gifts.

It is not simply a matter
Of handing out money,
Food, or equipment.
It calls
For more than that.
Our response
Is to share who we are
As well as what we have.
We are invited
To be fully and actively involved
In all areas
Of human activity and development,
Education, medicine, agriculture,
Craftwork and building.
We are the carpenters,
The catechists, the nurses,
The community builders, the doctors
And the farmers.
These are the skills
With which we have been blessed,
The talents
Which we have received.
We are not to bury them
But to freely share them
So that people might live
And be helped to reach
Their full human potential.
It is not a matter
Of charity or good deeds.
It is a basic Christian obligation
To justice.
What we have to offer
Is what we have been freely given.

We live with the people
We suffer with the people
We rejoice with the people
We become part of the people.
Our sharing becomes
A journey we walk together
Towards liberation
And a reaching out together for
Growth and fulfillment.

But we do not impose ourselves
Or our way of doing things.
We are at the service of.
We are the servants.
This means that
We are available
To go wherever we are invited
In the world.
It presupposes an openness
To the needs of others
And a spirit
Of confidence and poverty.

This spirit of poverty
Makes itself available
As fertile ground open
To whatever fruit the Lord
Wishes to plant.
We may never see
The results of our work.
If we truly follow
The way of Christ
We will find the Cross
As well as the Resurrection.

The Path of Jesus
Which we freely choose to follow
Has no trace
Of glory or honor or pomp.
It calls for a confidence and faith
And looks for nothing
Beyond that.

We are aware that
Through our service
We receive far more than
We are ever able to give.
We realize that
We are enriched
By our encounter
With people of other cultures and beliefs.
We come to discover
That we too are poor in many ways
And need to grow
Through receiving from those
To whom we go.
Our work
Entails human relationship
Working and growing together
To build a more
Humane and loving world
Filled with the Spirit of God
Who sends us.

Our mission is never complete.
It is an ongoing challenge
Calling us to continual growth.

We, the People of God,
Do not establish the Kingdom,
We work towards it
In faith and hope.
We see that we are part
Of a Church which
Is a human institution
Struggling to respond
To its mission
And ever in need
Of growth and renewal.
We go
As representatives of our local churches
To share the gifts we have.
We are in solidarity
With the church that sends us
And have a commitment
To return
And share the gifts and riches
Which we have received.
Our task is then
To continue our work as missionaries
In our own home countries.
We have a prophetic task
To help renew and invigorate
Our own church
For we recognize
Our own needs, inadequacies, and hunger.
We see that mission
Is not a one-way process
Coming from a "First World Church,"
And ending with
A "Third World Church,"

But it is a cyclical process
Going from one church
To another church
In continuous, mutual sharing.
This is the dynamic of mission.
It is never static.
It is ever moving,
Ever growing and
Ever calling forth
The gifts and life in the other.
We recognize
The fire and dynamic power
Of the Holy Spirit in mission
Which cannot be contained by,
Or monopolized within,
Any human institution
But which is at work
Where She wills.
We see the Spirit at work
In those to whom we go
As well as within ourselves;
We are channels of the Spirit,
Called forth to renew and strengthen
And be renewed and strengthened
In return.
VMM missionaries are open
To this dynamic and free action
Of the Spirit
Who first inspired and called us
To the service of the Lord.

VMM missionaries are
Followers of Jesus
Engaged fully
In the mission of the Church
Through active service in the world.

We praise and bless the Lord
Who calls us to live and to be
In the world
And to share his mission
Of love and peace
With all men and women
Of every color, race, and belief.